It's Overtaking Us
Μας προσπερνά

Aristea Papalexandrou
Translation by Philip Ramp

Fomite
Burlington, Vermont

Copyright © 2020 Aristea Papalexandrou
Translations copyright © 2020 Philip Ramp
Cover image - Detail from *Marine*, Gustave Courbet, 1866

All rights reserved. No part of this book may be reproduced in any form or by any means without the prior written consent of the publisher, except in the case of brief quotations used in reviews and certain other noncommercial uses permitted by copyright law.

ISBN-78-1-944388-62-1
Library of Congress Control Number: 2019945009

Fomite
58 Peru Street
Burlington, VT 05401
www.fomitepress.com

ΠΕΡΙΕΧΟΜΕΝΑ

Περνούν οι μέρες	2
Αντιδάνεια	4
Δραπέτισσα (Σταδίου)	8
Δραπέτισσα (Ομήρου και Σαχτούρη)	10
Ο αυτόπτης	14
Placebo	16
Ωδή στον οδοιπόρο	18
Όνειρο ανίδωτο	20
Λευκό ανεξίτηλο	24
Φυλάτε τα νώτα σας	28
Άνεμος το φυσά	30
Τα ροζ μιας αεικίνητης κυρίας	32
Ρέκβιεμ για τον νεκρό που ομόρφυνε	36
Άρπαξ ημέρα	38
Στέλνει θλίψη	40
Πρωτοχρονιά	42
Αναισθησιογόνο	44
Όποιος φοβάται την άνοιξη	46
Τα εξ αδιαιρέτου (Εν Πηλίω στοιχειωμένα)	48
Το μισθωτήριο	52
Όσοι μείναν	54
Εαρινή προβολή	56
Τί ώρα έρχεται;	62
Ολοκαίνουργιο	64
Εις εαυτόν	68
Είναι κάτι δίχως	72

Contents

Introductory Note By Kiki Dimoula	1
The days go by	3
Inverted Loans	5
The Fugitive (Stadiou St.)	9
The Fugitive (Corner of Omirou and Sachtouri Sts.)	11
Eyewitness	15
Placebo	17
Ode To The Wayfarer	19
Dream Unbeheld	21
Indelible White	25
Mind your back	29
Wind Its Blowing	31
The Pink Hues Of A Lady In Perpetual Motion	33
Requiem For The Dead Man Who Grew More Beautiful	37
The Day Seizes	39
Sends sorrow	41
New Year's	43
Anestheisiologon	45
Whoever fears spring	47
Ab Indivisio (Haunted on Pelion)	49
The Lease	53
All those left	55
Springtime Projection	57
When Is It Coming?	63
Brand New	65
To Oneself	69
It's something void of how void of what	73
Notes	75

Introductory Note By Kiki Dimoula*

Even in her earliest books, Aristea's Papalexandrou's work was notable for having a voice all its own; her poetry, metrical at times, as an offshoot of free verse
showed she was serving tradition successfully. So it is not by chance that particular attention was paid to her second book, *Once, Elsewhere*, and not only by the critics but—limited as it may be—the poetry reading public, if one can judge by the fact it was on the list of best selling books in the largest Greek newspapers.

Two poetry collections were to follow: *Songbirds* and *Underground*: both examples of a style stripped of all ornament, and even though its strong sense of irony is connected to a degree to K.P. Cavafy's or Kostas Karyotakis' work, it has also transformed that into a completely modern narrative on the absurdity of our period, as it's set forth by an apparently uninvolved observer from "observation posts" chosen by the poet from among those used by her worthy ancestors.

At the end of 2015 her fifth collection of poetry, *It's Overtaking Us*, was published, clearly showing her maturity has made an even further advance. Again, existential unease is prominent, coupled with her ironical manner of expression —mockingly at times, even self-mockingly at other times as well. But in *It's Overtaking Us*, the multi-layered, abstract style is structured with even greater rigor showing it to be indubitably the work of Aristea Papalexandrou, making her thus one of the most important representatives of her poetic generation.

As critics have rightly observed: this poet works, in the final analysis, on a dialectical basis: the poem "To Oneself", directed to an absent you, exemplifies her ability to create hypothetical

dialogues, a current that runs strongly throughout her work. And, of course, this dialogue, as a poetic mode, is immediately shown to be with none other than the reader himself who, in the end, remains part of the poet's space, a participant in what *It's Overtaking Us* is so attempting to achieve:

> *It's something void of*
> *how void of what*
> *while living it*
> *consumes you bit-by-bit.*

Περνούν οι μέρες
μικραίνει η ζωή
και ποιο φως
ποιο σκοτάδι θ' αντέξει

The days go by
life gets shorter
and which light
which darkness will endure

Αντιδάνεια

> *Ένας Θεός γεννιέται. Άλλοι πεθαίνουν. Η Αλήθεια*
> *ούτε έφυγε ούτε ήρθε: το Λάθος άλλαξε.*
> Φερνάντο Πεσσόα

Κι όμως το παραδέχομαι
δεν είναι τωρινό κακό.
Δεκαετίες έπλεκα ατέλειωτα
μνημόσυνα εν μέσω
μνημονίων· τί το καινούργιο;
Το λάθος μου δεν άλλαξε.
Με τρέφει ληξιπρόθεσμο
μα εγώ ούτε λέξη άσχετη

δεν του αποταμιεύω.

Η προθεσμία έληξε.
Το ξέρουν και το ξέρω.
Επίορκη από καιρό
εξαργυρώνω κάθιδρη
ως και τη σιωπή μου:
λυγμό ασυνάρτητον ηχώ
πριν απ' τον δύσκολο καιρό
πριν απ' τη γέννησή μου.

Η προθεσμία έληξε.
              Μαζί κι εγώ.
Το λάθος μου δεν άλλαξε

Inverted Loans

> *A God is born. Others die. The Truth*
> *neither departed nor arrived: The Error changed*
> Fernando Pessoa

Nevertheless I accept
it's not a current evil.
Decades I spent weaving
endless commemorations via
memorandums; so what's new?
My error did not change.
What falls due nourishes me
but not one irrelevant word do

I set aside for it.

The deadline passed.
They know it and I know it.
Perjurer for some time
Soaked in sweat I profit
right down to my silence:
sound of an incoherent sob
before the difficult time
before my birth.

The deadline passed.
          Me with it.
My error did not change

δανείστηκε αυτουργό.
Κι εγώ στου κόσμου το κακό
ένταλμα ανεξόφλητο
πετώ την ενοχή μου.

a wrongdoer borrowing.
And I amid the world's evil
an unpaid voucher
tossing my guilt away.

Δραπέτισσα (Σταδίου)

μούσα πολύτροπον...

Την ξέρω αυτήν την άγνωστη
Από το φως που άπλωνε
το μαύρο φόρεμά της

Θά 'λεγα απ' την ανάποδη
κι εκείνη πως με ξέρει
Νιώθω σαν να με παρακολουθεί
απ' τον καιρό που ασθμαίνουσα
τριγύριζα στην πόλη
Κι άκουγα λες και από μακριά
στο αυτί μου την σιωπή της:
«Άλαλη αντίζηλος γλιστρά
με φόρα στην Σταδίου»

Άλαλη αντίζηλος εγώ
Κι ορθώνεται μπροστά μου

Ωραία η νεαρά σιωπή
Με ξέρει και την ξέρω
Εγώ κι εκείνη
άσαρκη
στο μαύρο μου φουστάνι
Σαν κάτι θέλει να μου πει
Με τρώει για να με τρέφει
Γλυκά εισχωρεί στο είναι μου

Την τρέφω και με τρέφει.

The Fugitive[1] (Stadiou St.)

muse ingenious...

I know this stranger
By the light spread by
her black dress

I should put it the other way round
it's she who knows me
I feel like she's been following me
since the time when gasping
I wandered about the city
And I heard as if from afar
her silence in my ear:
"Speechless rival slip
into Stadiou swiftly"

I the speechless rival
And it rises before me

Lovely this youthful silence
It knows me and I know it
I and her
fleshless
in my black dress
As if she wants to tell me something
Consuming me to feed me
Sweetly permeating my being

I feed her and she feeds me.

Δραπέτισσα (Ομήρου και Σαχτούρη)

I

[Ωραία ως άστατη]

Απ' τους δρόμους που
πέρασα πέρασε
Παρελαύνει κι αλλάζει
φορέματα χρώματα
Ντεφιλέ καταστρώνει
    στων αιώνων
      τη ράχη
Παρελαύνει κι αλλάζει
    μορφή.

II

[Ωραία ως διάβολος]

Με ωθεί σ' ελαφρά
    παραπτώματα:
Κάνω δήθεν πως ξέχασα
    πρόσωπα
Μικρές τύψεις
    γεννιούνται μεμιάς
και σε λίγο πεθαίνουν
    μικρότερες.

The Fugitive (Corner of Omirou and Sachtouri Sts.)

      I

[Beauty as in caprice]

The streets I passed
she passed too
Parading by and changing
dresses colors
Presenting a fashion show
    on the back
    of the ages
Parading by and changing
    form.

      II

[Beauty as in devilish]

She shoves me I stumble
    slightly:
I act like I've forgotten
    faces
Minor qualms
    are born of a sudden
die after awhile
    more trivial yet.

III

[Ωραία ως άγγελος]

Με θωπεύει
το γκρίζο απ' το μαύρο
παλτό που ανεμίζει
        στον ήλιο της.

IV

[Ωραία ως μούσα]

Μου μιλά κι αφουγκράζομαι
ό,τι χρειάζεται για να σβήσω
μια λέξη σε γλώσσα νεκρή
        Μια εποχή.

V

Την γνωρίζω.
Είναι κάπου Ομήρου
και Σαχτούρη γωνία
Ακούγεται:

Δεν έχω γράψει ποιήματα.

Αλήθεια λέει. Εκείνη
λέξη ποτέ δεν έγραψε.

Υ.Γ.: Η πιο γνωστή σας άγνωστη
σαν κάτι πάει να ξαναπεί
και πάλι δραπετεύει.

III

[Beauty as in angel)

I'm caressed
by the grey from the black
coat that flutters
      in her sun.

IV

(Beauty as in muse)

She speaks to me and I strain to hear
as much as needed to erase
one word from a dead language
      An epoch.

V

I know her
She's somewhere on the corner
of Omirou and Sachtouri Sts.
There is heard:

I have not written poems.[2]

She's telling the truth. She's
never written a single word.

PS. Your most well-known unknown person
is like someone about to speak again
before fleeing once more.

Ο αυτόπτης

Στο λευκό του
πουκάμισο κλειδωμένος
είναι κάτι στιγμές βραδινές
που περνά αστραπή από μπρος μου
και χάνεται λες και σβήνει
πριν μου γνέψει
πως έφυγε
        φεύγει

Ξέρω λίγα γι' αυτόν ασυνάρτητα
Δεν είναι από δω
και δεν είναι για κάτι σπουδαίος
Όμως έχει έναν τρόπο να πείθει
Αξιόπιστος ξένος· τον επέλεξαν
αλλουνού την υπόσχεση ν' αθετήσει
Άνθρωπος δίκαιος δανεικής
        ενοχής
Ίσως θά 'θελε νά 'χε
μιλήσει κι αυτός για κείνη
        τη νύχτα
Για των άλλων το άλλοθι
Όσα είδε καθώς πήγαινε
        ερχόταν
εισχωρώντας στο βήμα τους

Αυτός ο άνθρωπος βουβός
με προστάζει ν' αρθρώσω
        φωνή

Eyewitness (3)

Locked in
his white shirt
there are some twilight moments
when he flashes before my eyes
is lost, you'd think erased
before he nods at me
that he'd left
        he's leaving

The little I know about him is inconsistent
He's not from here
and is not in any sense important
But he does have a way of being convincing
Trustworthy stranger; they chose him
to breach the promise of another
True man of borrowed
        guilt
Perhaps he would like to
have spoken himself about
        that night
About the others' alibi
All he saw as he was passing by
        coming
infiltrating their steps

This mute human
commanding me to articulate
        voice

Placebo

Δεν πρόλαβα· ίσως και να μην
      ήθελα
Το σώμα πλέον αδρανεί
κι αυτό που στάζει τον λυγμό
λέξη προς λέξη στο χαρτί
Αυτό το ψευδοφάρμακο
της πρώτης γόνιμης αυγής
      πολύ μακριά μου
Δώρο που δεν μου
δώρισε καμιά
      συνέχειά μου

Placebo

I didn't make it; maybe I didn't want
        to
the body now inert
it's the sob dripping
word by word on paper
This pseudo-medicine
of the first fertile dawn
        so very far from me
Gift that has never
given me any
continuity at all

Ωδή στον οδοιπόρο

Φορώντας το άγγιγμά της
κατέφθασε ανοιξιάτικος
και ως άλλος μου συστήθηκε.
Όσο να πεις, ακόμα ακμαίος.
Όμως δεν παύει νά 'ναι αυτός
άλλοτε ολότελα δικός μου
προτού ραγίσει αθόρυβος
στη μετακόμιση οδός
Εσφιγμενίτου 12.

Τώρα δεν μένει πια εκεί.
Κι ίσως δεν μένει πουθενά.
Φορώντας το άγγιγμά της προχωρεί
λες και πλανιέται με σκοπό μοναδικό
ως άλλος ξένος να μου ξανα-
συστηθεί.

Ode To The Wayfarer

Dressed in her touch
and spring-like he overtook me
and as another was introduced to me.
Whatever you may say, he's still thriving,
Indeed never stopped being who he is
once completely mine
till he cracked soundlessly
in the move to 12
Esfigmenitou St.

He no longer lives there.
And perhaps not anywhere.
Dressed in her touch he proceeds
you'd think his wandering had a single purpose
to be reintroduced to me as yet
another stranger.

Όνειρο ανίδωτο

> *Δέδυκε μὲν ἀ σελάννα*
> *καὶ Πληίαδες· μέσαι δὲ*
> *νύκτες, παρὰ δ' ἔρχετ' ὤρα·*
> *ἔγω δὲ μόνα κατεύδω.*
> Σαπφώ

Σε λίμνης όχθη
πολύ παλιά
ένα ζευγάρι θάφτηκε
τόσο κοντά
σαν να 'ταν ένα σώμα

Κανείς δεν έμαθε ποτέ
τον λόγο του θανάτου
Απ' των απόντων την σιωπή
κάποιοι πλέξαν στα δάχτυλα
και μύθο και ιστορία

Λουόμενοι στο ασήμι της νυκτός
Δύο ψυχές ο κόσμος όλος
στιλπνό γλυπτό
Αυτός και αυτή

Κανείς δεν έμαθε ποιοι ήταν
ο κόσμος λίκνο
μιανής σαρκός
Αυτός και αυτή

Ώσπου ξεφλούδισαν τη γη
μεγάλες ξηρασίες
Βότσαλα ψήγματα χρυσού
φέγγισαν στο σκοτάδι
και το ζευγάρι ολόγυμνο

Dream Unbeheld

> *Moon gone from the sky*
> *lost in the Pleiades*
> *midnight and time slipping by*
> *while I lie here alone*
> Sappho

On a lakeshore
so very long ago
a couple was buried
so tight to one another
it was like one body

No one ever learned
the reason for this death
From the silence of the missing
some twined myth and
history on their fingers

Bathed in night's silver
Two souls a world entire
lustrous sculpture
Him and her

No one ever learned who they were
the world a cradle
of one flesh
Him and her

Until the earth was stripped bare
by great droughts
Pebbles specks of gold
gleamed in the dark

δίχως πληγές ούτε αμυχή
ευθυτενής διάθλαση
στο στρογγυλό φεγγάρι
που τους κοιτάζει

που με κοιτάζει
με τιμωρεί

που ο κόσμος όλος
εσύ

and the couple stark naked
without wounds not a scratch
erect refraction
on the round moon
looking at them

which looking at me
punishes me

that the whole world
you

Λευκό ανεξίτηλο

Αυτό πάλι πώς το
    εξηγείς
Νά 'χεις σπίτι σου τόσα
μολύβια στυλό
μαρκαδόρους
μπλοκ σκορπισμένα
πενάκια χαρτάκια
σελίδες Α4
post-it κόλες
αναφοράς
ραπιδογράφους
Τόσα άθικτα αναλώσιμα
όλα μπροστά σου
λες και προστάζουν να τα δεις
κάπου να χρησιμέψουν

Κι όταν έρχεται αυτή η
    μεγάλη στιγμή
πώς το εξηγείς
που τίποτα δεν βρίσκεις
μια λέξη έστω μια συλλαβή

Όχι πως θα τη συγκρατήσεις
Μάταιος κόπος. Μικρή ή
μεγάλη πέρασε πάει
Μια νέα άπιαστη
στιγμή ευθύς θα σε ρουφήξει

Πέρασε πάει α-
στόχησες
το παρελθόν της να

Indelible White

Once again just how can you
        explain
Having in your house so many
pencils pens
felt-tip pens
notebooks scattered about
nibs bits of paper
sheets of A4
post-its stickers examination
sheets
stenographic pens
So many untouched consumer items
all there before you
as if commanding you to look at them
make use of them somewhere

And when that great moment
        does come
how will you explain
not finding a thing
not a word even a syllable

It's not you'll hold on to it
Wasted effort. Minor or
major it's over gone
A new elusive
moment will swallow you straightaway

It's over gone you were off-
target
you violated her

αθετήσεις
μ' ένα στυλό που στέρεψε
το πιέζεις και δεν
γράφει

      past
with a pen that ran dry
you bear down but it won't
write

Φυλάτε τα νώτα σας
μη μαγέψει η χαρά την ψυχή
κι ευθύς λησμονήσετε
πολέμους και μάχες

Mind your back
so joy will not soul enthrall
so you at once forget
wars and battles

Άνεμος το φυσά

Αυτός ο άνθρωπος
στα θολά ανεβαίνει
μια γυάλινη σκάλα
Κρατά μαύρο περίστροφο
πυρπολεί στον αέρα
εκβιάζει τα σύννεφα
να χιονίσει
Δεν τον βλέπεις συνήθως
με μάτι γυμνό
Τον σκαρώνουν τα άρρωστα
μάτια μυώπων
Οπτασία θα πεις
στο κενό των ανέμων

Και μετά... Να τος σάρκινος
καθιστός σε συμβούλια
Ημερήσια Διάταξη
και είσαι μέσα κι εσύ
σωτηρίας παράδειγμα
Σε καλεί να ανέβεις τη σκάλα
τρέμεις... άνεμος σε φυσά
Μα επιμένεις

Κι όταν πας να πατήσεις
το πρώτο σκαλί επανέρχεσαι
Δέκα δέκατα όραση
κι ένα βήμα γκρεμός
η αλήθεια
μπροστά σου

Wind Its Blowing

This man
is climbing a glass
stairway in mist
He's holding a black revolver
shooting into the air
forcing the clouds
to snow
You ordinarily can't see him
with the naked eye
Eyes suffering from myopia
concoct him
An apparition you'd say
in the winds' void

And then... There he is in the flesh
sitting in committees
The Day's Agenda
and you're there as well
example of redemption
He invites you to climb the stairs
you're trembling... wind blowing on you
But you persist

And just as you're set to step
you're back at the first rung
10/10 vision
the abyss but a stride away
the truth
before you

Τα ροζ μιας αεικίνητης κυρίας

I

Δεν τέλειωσε, θα πεις.
Δεν έγραψα
το ποίημα της επιστροφής.
Δεν έγραψα κανένα ποίημα.

Όμως ο χρόνος γύρισε
ρότα σε άλλο ψέμα.
Ούτε ξεχνάς ούτε ξεχνώ.
Ούτε νικάς ούτε νικώ.
Των τέως λάγνων ημερών
πλήρης ισοπαλία.
Έως εδώ.

II

Κάποιος σε λίγο αναχωρεί.
Επείγεται να είσαι
εσύ με αυτήν την
αεικίνητη κυρία.
Το ξέρω την ακολουθείς.
Ίσως και να την φτάσεις.

Κάποιος σε λίγο αποχωρεί.

The Pink Hues Of A Lady In Perpetual Motion

I

It's not finished, you'll say.
I didn't write
the poem of return.
I didn't write any poem.

However time passed
on course to another lie.
You haven't forgotten nor I.
You haven't won nor I.
At the end of lascivious days
a dead heat.
To here.

II

Soon someone will be departing
It's urgent that you
be with this
lady in perpetual motion.
I know you're following her.
Perhaps you'll catch up.

Soon someone will be departing.

Επείγεται να είμαι εγώ
πες για τον δίσεκτο καιρό
τον βυθισμένο στο σκοτάδι
γι' αυτούς τους άνυδρους αγρούς
τις άγονες κοιλάδες
τους πένητες των πόλεων
εν πάση συγκυρία.
Για την αλήθεια τελικά.

Αυτήν την αεικίνητη κυρία.

It's urgent I do too
let's say to an unlucky time
the one sunken in darkness
for those drought-stricken fields
those barren valleys
those left penniless in cities
by coincidence.
For the truth in the end.

This lady in perpetual motion.

Ρέκβιεμ για τον νεκρό που ομόρφυνε

Πάνω στα ειπωμένα
θα ειπωθεί και αυτό
μιας ληξιπρόθεσμης πληγής
το πρακτικό.

Έφτασε η ώρα της απογραφής
έμψυχα κι άψυχα
της περασμένης μας κοινής
ζωής όλα
τα καταγράφω
Στα δάχτυλά μου σε κρατώ
σκυφτόν
Σε σφίγγω κι ευθύς
Νάρκισσο
σ' ελευθερώνω
Απ' το ρομάντζο μας
ούτε έναν στίχο δεν κρατώ
Έναν επίλογο σωστό
δεν έγραψα
και ούτε

Requiem For The Dead Man Who Grew More Beautiful

On top of what's been said
this too will be said
the proceedings
on an injury that fell due.

The time has come for stock-taking
animate and inanimate
I'm recording
all the past we shared
in common
I'm holding you in my fingers
bent over
I squeeze you and like that
Narcissus
I free you
I am not keeping a single verse
from our romance
didn't write
a proper epilogue
not even

Άρπαξ ημέρα

Σαν από λάθος τρύπωσα
σε μίας άλλης ζωντανής
την ιστορία

Την διαδέχτηκα καθώς
κοιμόταν ελαφρά
βίον ευτυχισμένο
Δεν ήξερα για τη ζωή της
τίποτα
Ξύπνησα απλώς ένα πρωί
πλησίον τινός αγνώστου

Ο ρόλος μου άγραφος
λευκό χαρτί
Σε μένα έγκειται
και να τον γράψω
και να τον ζήσω

Ξημέρωσε
χρεόγραφο κενό
Έστω κλεμμένη μέρα
επείγεται να την
ρουφήξω

The Day Seizes

As if by accident I slotted myself
into the story of another
living human being

I gave way to her as
she was sleeping lightly
a happy life
I knew nothing about her
life
I simply awoke one morning
next to a stranger

My role is white paper
not written on
It's incumbent on me
to both write it
and live it

Day broke
blank security
Though the day's stolen
it's urgent I
swallow it

Στέλνει θλίψη
μια μικρή σπιθαμή
κι ώρα σ' ώρα
κατακλύζει τον κόσμο

Sends sorrow
tiniest of spans
moment by moment
it's inundating the world

Πρωτοχρονιά

Από τα ξένα θίασοι
μας ήρθαν
        μας ακούστηκαν
                μας φύγαν.

Ώρα ενδεκάτη άγρυπνη
οδεύει το άστυ αφώτιστο στην
        δωδεκάτη.
Μαρμαρωμένο βασιλόψωμο
καλεί το αφόρετο μεταξωτό μιας
        Ιοκάστης
Καλή χρονιά και *Καληνύχτα*.

Μνήμες στοιβάζονται στιγμές
Δύο χιλιάδες δέκα...
Νέας χρονιάς
ξημέρωμα το μέλλον
μάς λιγόστεψε.

Νύχτα βουβή.

New Year's

Troupes came to us
from abroad
        listened to us
                left us.

Eleven o'clock sleepless
the unlit city heading for
        twelve
Vassilopsomo[4] petrified
calls to mind the unworn silk of a
        Jocasta
Happy New Year and *Goodnight*.

Memories piled in moments
Two thousand and ten...
New year
dawn our diminishing
future.

Mute night.

Αναισθησιογόνο

Παραθυρόφυλλα ανοιχτά
κανένα όμως παράθυρο
στο βάθος.
Κοιμήθηκαν πολύ βαριά
τα σύντομα όνειρά μου
και ξύπνησαν γιγάντιες
Άρπυιες εφιάλτες.

Εκεί στο αόρατο κενό
μου γνέφουν να παραιτηθώ.
Μα εγώ θα βρω την
      έξοδο.
Κι όχι, δεν θα 'μαι
μοναχή. Θ' ακούω τη
      φωνή μου.
Σωστά σε ηχογράφησαν ηχώ
της σιωπής μου.

Anestheisiologon

Shutters open
but no window
behind.
My brief dreams
slept very heavily
and woke gigantic
Harpies' nightmares.

There in the invisible abyss
they signal me to give up.
But I will find the
        exit.
And no, I won't be
alone. I will hear
        my voice.
Correctly, in the recorded sound
of my silence.

Όποιος φοβάται την άνοιξη
μπρος στον χειμώνα να σταθεί

Whoever fears spring
will come to a halt faced with winter

Τα εξ αδιαιρέτου
(Εν Πηλίω στοιχειωμένα)

Δεν ήρθε για κανέναν κατοικήσιμο
αυτό το καλοκαίρι
Όσο για τη βδομάδα αυτήν
των συναντήσεων
ξέπλυνε συγκινήσεις
      αδηφάγες

Φιδίσιος δρόμος
ζεματιστός
κατολισθαίνοντας προς άπειρον
σκοτωμένα σκυλιά στην
      άσφαλτο
δύσκολη η σκέψη για νερό
δύσκολη η ανάσα

Κι όταν αντίκρισες
χλομός
τα πρώτα στοιχειωμένα
από καιρό ακατοίκητα
όλα σε φώναζαν
να ξεκλειδώσεις

Τη θάλασσα, τη θάλασσα
Ξεκλείδωσε τη θάλασσα

Διώροφα τριώροφα
άδεια στην ερημία
Όμως η πόρτα πουθενά
και το κλειδί σπασμένο

Ab Indivisio
(Haunted on Pelion)

This summer did not turn out
to be inhabitable for anyone
As for this week
of meetings
it flushed away ravenous
       emotions

Twisting road
scorching
sliding toward infinity
dogs smeared on the
       asphalt
hard to think about water
hard to breathe

And when wan you come
face to face
with the first haunted dwellings
vacant for years
they all cry out to you
to unlock

The sea, the sea
Unlock the sea

Two-story three-story
empty in a wasteland
Door nowhere to be found
and the key broken

Τη θάλασσα
Αλλιώς θα σε στερέψει
Διώροφα τριώροφα

Ούτε ένα κατοικήσιμο
να ζήσεις να το μοιραστείς
το άλλο καλοκαίρι

Η θάλασσα, η θάλασσα
πάλαι ποτέ ολάνθιστων
Πηλίων παραδείσων

Η θάλασσα από μακριά

Δεν θά 'ρθει για κανέναν
κατοικήσιμο το άλλο καλοκαίρι

The sea
Otherwise it will dry you up
Two-story three-story

Not one inhabitable
a place to live and share
the coming summer

The sea, the sea
a once upon a time Pelion
paradise in full flower

The sea from afar

The coming summer no one will
find anything inhabitable

Το μισθωτήριο

Κι ευθύς ζωή ξεπέρασες
ξανά τη φαντασία
Ώσπου ν' αλλάξω πλοηγό
σφάλισες κάθε δρόμο
Ούτε εκδρομή στ' ανθόφυτα
        λιβάδια του χειμώνα
Ούτε ταξίδι αναψυχής
        μέσα στον παγετώνα

Κι αναβολή σ' αναβολή
ξανά στη Δροσοπούλου
Να βγάζει σ' αδιέξοδο της λησμονιάς
ο κήπος για μια χρονιά
δύο χρονιές πεντέξι
δεκαπέντε
Δίχως ελπίδα να σε δω
ολάνθιστο σπιτάκι
Νά 'ναι η αλλαγή του σκηνικού
οριστικών απόντων
Μνημόσυνα
Χαρμόσυνα
στον λάκκο των
        λεόντων

The Lease

And your life gotten straightaway
back to fantasy again
Until I can change pilot
make sure every road is sealed
Not an excursion to flowering
      fields in winter
Not even a relaxing tour
      among glaciers

Postponement after postponement
back to Drosopoulos again
To extract the garden out of the dead
end of forgetfulness for a year
two years five six
fifteen
Without hope of seeing you my
flower-covered cottage
Let the change of scenery be
for the terminally missing
Memorials
Merriment
at the lions'
      den

Όσοι μείναν
παγετώνων φρουροί
και ήταν Μάιος

All those left
glacier guards
and it was May

Εαρινή προβολή

I

Ήταν σκοτεινιασμένος
ο ουρανός του ονείρου
Μετά ξημέρωσε
σκοτεινιασμένη μέρα

Άνδρες γυναίκες συρροή
αγνώστων συντροφίες
Αυτός ο κύριος αυτή
με τον λευκό λαιμό
Αυτός ο κύριος αυτή
—Με το μαύρο περίστροφο
Φιγούρες δίχως βλέμμα
μου γνέφουν μου μιλούν
Τους σέρνω όλους στη δουλειά
στη μυστική συνάντηση
με τον εντεταλμένο
του μεσιτικού στη γενική
συνέλευση στην εφορία
Πουλώ το βιος μου ξεπουλώ
σάλες γεμάτες τράπεζες
λαμπρές οινοποσίες

του ύπνου μου του ξύπνου μου
εμένα σώμα και ψυχή
υπάρχοντά μου όλα
με πουλώ με ξεπουλώ
υπάρχοντά μου
      παρελθόν

Springtime Projection

              I

Dream's sky
was overcast
Then an overcast day
broke as well

Men women a throng
companionship of strangers
This gentleman this
white throated woman
This man, her
—With the black revolver
Figures sightless
nodding at speaking to me
I'm dragging all of them off to work
to a secret meeting
with the one authorized
by the brokerage to the general
assembly to the tax office
I'm selling my life selling it off
salons tables packed in tight
resplendent libations

of my sleep my waking
me myself body and soul
all my belongings
I'm selling, selling myself off
my belongings
      past

αυτός με τον λευκό λαιμό
με το μαύρο περίστροφο
Φιγούρες
αεικίνητες
καλά κρυμμένα
μυστικά
γλίτωσαν όλοι
Κι ο δολοφόνος του φονιά
στο πιο ωραίο άλλοθι
μακριά στην Γουαδελούπη
Γλίτωσαν όλοι
πλην εμού
που τους ονειρευόμουν

II

Έως εδώ το όνειρο
και τώρα η προφητεία

Ύπνοι χωρίς ενύπνια
Φθινόπωρο χωρίς βροχή
Τσιγάρο στον ακάλυπτο
Γυμνή το καταχείμωνο
Κανείς να μη ζεσταίνεται
Κανείς να μην κρυώνει
Από παντού να βρέχεσαι
Από παντού να καίγεσαι
Άθικτος όπως πριν
Να παραμένεις

Ώστε
δεν είμαι μόνη,

the man with the white throat
with the black revolver
Figures
perpetually moving
well hidden
secrets
everyone was saved
And the assassin of the murderer
the most beautiful alibi
far away in Guadeloupe
Everyone was saved
except me
who was dreaming of them

    II

The dream up to here
from here on prophecy

Sleep without dream
Autumn without rain
Cigarette out in the open
Her naked, dead of winter
No one not getting warm
No one not getting cold
You're rained on from all sides
You're seared on all sides
Remaining untouched as
You were before

Therefore
I am not alone,

καλά το είπες
Και προπαντός
που δεν περίμενες
ο κόσμος σου να φωτιστεί
από έναν κάποιο ήλιο

you were right
And in any case
when you least expect it
your world is illuminated
by some kind of sun

Τί ώρα έρχεται;

Μίλησαν προφητείες παλιές
για το τέλος του κόσμου
Προχθές ώρα μεσημβρινή
σαν ορισμένη συγκοπή καρδίας

Ούτε ένας δεν τις πίστεψε
ούτε κι εγώ που
ουδόλως ντύθηκα στα μαύρα
επίσημα να δω το τέλος
να τελειώσω

Λοιπόν
δεν χρειάζεται
να λήξεις, κόσμε
Δεν χρειάζομαι την έκλειψή σου
για να εκλείψω

          Δεκ. του '12

When Is It Coming?

Old prophecies were speaking
about the end of the world
Day before yesterday midday
like a half-hearted heart attack

Not one of them didn't believe them
not even me who
in no case ever wore formal
black to see the end
I am ending

So
there is no need
to expire, I don't
need you people to vanish
to vanish myself

                                      December, 2012

Ολοκαίνουργιο

ἄριστον μὲν ὕδωρ
Πίνδαρος

Γυναίκα διέσχιζε ξυπόλυτη
την αποξηραμένη λίμνη
Κατρακυλώντας κατηφόριζε
να βρει πυθμένα
να στερεωθεί
Όμως πυθμένας δεν φαινόταν πουθενά
μόνο αχανής προοπτική του

Κι όλο σκεφτόταν πρόφαση
για να γυρίσει πίσω
—πως είναι ασήκωτα ελαφριά
μια τέτοια κατηφόρα
πως πόδια δεν αισθάνεται
κουράστηκε
και πως ως φαίνεται
πυθμένας δεν υπάρχει
Κι όλο την κάθε πρόφαση
σε λίγο έβγαζε ψεύτρα
Βάδιζε κι αναπτέρωνε
τα ψάρια της ερήμου
Βάδιζε κι αναπτέρωνε
και την απούσα εμένα

Κι όλο την ψεύτρα πρόφαση
έβγαζε πάλι ψεύτρα

Στο βάθος προχωρεί
και προχωρεί

Brand New

> *Water best of all*
> Pindar

A barefoot woman crossed over
the dry lake
She came tumbling down
trying to find a bottom
to steady herself on
But no bottom to be seen anywhere
only its immense prospect

And everything considered a pretext
for going back
—that it's unliftably light
with such a downhill slope
that she can't feel her feet
and became exhausted
and that it appears
there is no bottom
And each of her pretexts
soon made her out a liar
She strode and raised
fish from the desert
She strode and raised
my absent self as well

And that false pretext
made her a liar again

Into depth advancing
and advancing

για να μην φτάσει —
Αχανές κοίλωμα άνυδρο
από απουσία και χάος
τόπος προορισμού
δεν γίνεται να γίνει

Και δεν αναπτερώνονται μ' ένα κορμί
χωρίς κορμί νεκροί βυθοί
κι όστρακα στοιχειωμένα
σαν την ξυπόλυτη
                που όλο με προσπερνά
και λες ότι μου μοιάζει

Και δεν αφυδατώνομαι απ' όνειρο παλιό
Απ' αύριο ολοκαίνουργιον
συνθέτω εφιάλτη

so she'll never arrive —
Vast dry cavity
of absence and chaos
site of a destination
not destined to be achieved

And they are not roused with a body
without a body those deep dead
and haunted shells
like the barefoot woman
              who is relentlessly overtaking me
and you'd say she resembled me

And I am not being dehydrated by an old dream
Starting tomorrow I will be composing
a brand new nightmare

Εις εαυτόν

Το αίσθημα προπάντων
υψηλό
Δεν λέω, πέρασαν στιγμές
που ευθύς σας χλώμιασαν
Αρίστη
Άφησε η χλωμάδα σας
κενό στην πρώτη θέση
Το τρένο όμως κι αν πέρασε
και πάλι θα περάσει
Όχι, δεν έρχεται για σας
απλώς το συνηθίζει

Όποιος σταθεί στο στέγαστρο
ίσως
    μες στη ζωή του κλειδωθεί
—λίγων δεκάδων χιλιομέτρων
ασφυξία—
Έως εκεί
των βιωμένων σας στιγμών
η απεραντοσύνη

Όλα της γης τα πλάσματα
τόσο εν δυνάμει ελεύθερα
Ελεύθερη κι εσείς
και δεν επείγεσθε διά της γραφής
να διαιτάσθε
Απ' τα άγραφα στιχάκια σας
ούτε η ζωή σας σώζεται
ούτε ο θάνατός σας.

Το αίσθημα προπάντων

To Oneself

Above all else feeling is
high
Not to say there weren't moments
that straightaway made you blanch
Aristi[5]
Leave your paleness
empty in first class
But the train even though it's gone by
will be passing through again
No, it won't be coming for you
it's simply what it does

Whoever has stood under a shelter has
perhaps
        been locked into his life
—a few dozen kilometers
of suffocation —
Up to there
the infinity
of your living moments

All the creatures of earth
as free as possible
You too as free
and not pressured to support
yourself by your writing
Neither your life
nor you death is saved
by your unwritten verses.

Above all else feeling is

υψηλό
κι αυτό το ποίημα ατέλειωτο
κι αυτό δικό σας.

high
and this poem is endless
and this is yours.

Είναι κάτι δίχως
πώς δίχως τί
που όσο ζει
λίγο-λίγο σε λιώνει

It's something void of
how void of what
while living it
consumes you bit-by-bit

Notes

*Kiki Dimoula is considered by many as the greatest Greek poet of her generation or sharing that honor with Katerina Anghelaki-Rooke. Born in 1931 she has produced 16 volumes of poetry at last count while for many years holding a full time position at the Bank of Greece. She has been translated into many languages and received numerous awards among them the Greek State Prize (1971, 1988), the Kostas and Eleni Ouranis Prize (1994) and the Grand Prize for Literature (2001) the highest honor of the Academy of Athens of which she is also a member. In 2009 she was, in addition, awarded the European Prize for Literature.

1. The poet mentioned to the translator the Greek title was in some sense inspired by *The Fugitive (Albertine disparue...)* section of Proust's *Remembrance of Things Past* and though the poem is not directly related to it there is a sense of ambiguity, the sense of being lost, of being forgotten, a "fugitive" becoming estranged from even him or herself.

2. In Part V of the "The Fugitive" (Corner of Omirou and Sachtouri Sts.), the line *"I Have not written poems"* is taken from the poem "The Soldier Poet" by Miltos Sachtouris

3. In this poem there is an obvious conversation between Papalexandrou and George Seferis one that is carried on in "Wind, Its Blowing" and "Ab Indivisio". More specifically, in "Eyewitness" the poem "Narrative" by Seferis is the center of the conversation while in "Ab Indivisio" it's "K. Andromeda" from the collection "Mythistorima" .

4. Vassilopsomo is a special bread in a round loaf baked for

New Year's and named after St. Basil (Vassily), whose name day is January 1.

5. "Aristi", is a version of the poet's name: Aristea, which in addition to being a name means superior, excellent, distinguished. Both forms can be used as women's names.

About the Author

Aristea Papalexandrou (b. 1970) has published 5 collections of poetry and her poems and essays on poetry and the theater have appeared in many Greek newspapers and literary magazines. She studied music and Medieval Modern Greek Philology. During the past two decades she has been involved with the investigation of the post-dictatorial period in Greece and its evaluation of the work of modern Greek female poets, a work which in March 2014 was deemed by the School of Fine Arts worthy of being used as her doctoral thesis under the title: *The Involvement with the Poetics of Female Creative Artists during the final quarter of the 20th Century.* She is also professionally involved with editing texts and typographic corrections while at the same time teaching The History of Modern Greek Literature at various cultural institutions. Her poetry has been put to music by the notable composers Michalis Kaloyerakis and Apostolos Kitsos. Finally, she was awarded the coveted Petros Haris Award of the Athens Academy for the collection *It's Overtaking Us* as well as her general contribution to Greek Literature.

About the Translator

Philip Ramp (b. 1940) was born in Michigan and attended the University of Michigan. He has lived in Greece for over 50 years (50 of them with his wife who recently died). He has published 15 collections of his own poetry and an equal number of collections of Greek poets in English translation. Both his poetry and his translations from the Greek have been published in the USA, UK and Greece.

About Fomite

A fomite is a medium capable of transmitting infectious organisms from one individual to another.

"The activity of art is based on the capacity of people to be infected by the feelings of others." Tolstoy, *What Is Art?*

Writing a review on Amazon, Good Reads, Shelfari, Library Thing or other social media sites for readers will help the progress of independent publishing. To submit a review, go to the book page on any of the sites and follow the links for reviews. Books from independent presses rely on reader to reader communications.

For more information or to order any of our books, visit http://www.fomitepress.com/

More Titles from Fomite...

Novels
Joshua Amses — *During This, Our Nadir*
Joshua Amses — *Ghatsr*
Joshua Amses — *Raven or Crow*
Joshua Amses — *The Moment Before an Injury*
Jaysinh Birjepatel — *Nothing Beside Remains*
Jaysinh Birjepatel — *The Good Muslim of Jackson Heights*
David Brizer — *Victor Rand*
Paula Closson Buck — *Summer on the Cold War Planet*
Dan Chodorkoff — *Loisaida*
David Adams Cleveland — *Time's Betrayal*
Jaimee Wriston Colbert — *Vanishing Acts*
Roger Coleman — *Skywreck Afternoons*
Marc Estrin — *Hyde*
Marc Estrin — *Kafka's Roach*
Marc Estrin — *Speckled Vanities*
Zdravka Evtimova — *In the Town of Joy and Peace*
Zdravka Evtimova — *Sinfonia Bulgarica*
Daniel Forbes — *Derail This Train Wreck*
Peter Fortunato — *Carnevale*
Greg Guma — *Dons of Time*
Richard Hawley — *The Three Lives of Jonathan Force*
Lamar Herrin — *Father Figure*
Michael Horner — *Damage Control*
Ron Jacobs — *All the Sinners Saints*
Ron Jacobs — *Short Order Frame Up*
Ron Jacobs — *The Co-conspirator's Tale*
Scott Archer Jones — *And Throw Away the Skins*
Scott Archer Jones — *A Rising Tide of People Swept Away*
Julie Justicz — *Degrees of Difficulty*
Maggie Kast — *A Free Unsullied Land*

Fomite

Darrell Kastin — *Shadowboxing with Bukowski*
Coleen Kearon — *#triggerwarning*
Coleen Kearon — *Feminist on Fire*
Jan English Leary — *Thicker Than Blood*
Diane Lefer — *Confessions of a Carnivore*
Rob Lenihan — *Born Speaking Lies*
Douglas Milliken — *Our Shadow's Voice*
Colin Mitchell — *Roadman*
Ilan Mochari — *Zinsky the Obscure*
Peter Nash — *Parsimony*
Peter Nash — *The Perfection of Things*
George Ovitt — *Stillpoint*
George Ovitt — *Tribunal*
Gregory Papadoyiannis — *The Baby Jazz*
Pelham — *The Walking Poor*
Andy Potok — *My Father's Keeper*
Frederick Ramey — *Comes A Time*
Joseph Rathgeber — *Mixedbloods*
Kathryn Roberts — *Companion Plants*
Robert Rosenberg — *Isles of the Blind*
Fred Russell — *Rafi's World*
Ron Savage — *Voyeur in Tangier*
David Schein — *The Adoption*
Lynn Sloan — *Principles of Navigation*
L.E. Smith — *The Consequence of Gesture*
L.E. Smith — *Travers' Inferno*
L.E. Smith — *Untimely RIPped*
Bob Sommer — *A Great Fullness*
Tom Walker — *A Day in the Life*
Susan V. Weiss — *My God, What Have We Done?*
Peter M. Wheelwright — *As It Is On Earth*
Suzie Wizowaty — *The Return of Jason Green*

Poetry
Anna Blackmer — *Hexagrams*
Antonello Borra — *Alfabestiario*
Antonello Borra — *AlphaBetaBestiaro*
Antonello Borra — *Fabbrica delle idee/The Factory of Ideas*
L. Brown — *Loopholes*
Sue D. Burton — *Little Steel*
Christine Butterworth-McDermott — *Evelyn As*
David Cavanagh — *Cycling in Plato's Cave*
James Connolly — *Picking Up the Bodies*
Greg Delanty — *Loosestrife*
Mason Drukman — *Drawing on Life*
J. C. Ellefson — *Foreign Tales of Exemplum and Woe*
Tina Escaja/Mark Eisner — *Caida Libre/Free Fall*
Anna Faktorovich — *Improvisational Arguments*
Barry Goldensohn — *Snake in the Spine, Wolf in the Heart*
Barry Goldensohn — *The Hundred Yard Dash Man*

Fomite

Barry Goldensohn — *The Listener Aspires to the Condition of Music*
R. L. Green — *When You Remember Deir Yassin*
Gail Holst-Warhaft — *Lucky Country*
Raymond Luczak — *A Babble of Objects*
Kate Magill — *Roadworthy Creature, Roadworthy Craft*
Tony Magistrale — *Entanglements*
Gary Mesick — *General Discharge*
Andreas Nolte — *Mascha: The Poems of Mascha Kaléko*
Sherry Olson — *Four-Way Stop*
Brett Ortler — *Lessons of the Dead*
Aristea Papalexandrou/Philip Ramp — Μας προσπερνά/*It's Overtaking Us*
Janice Miller Potter — *Meanwell*
Janice Miller Potter — *Thoreau's Umbrella*
Philip Ramp — *The Melancholy of a Life as the Joy of Living It Slowly Chills*
Joseph D. Reich — *A Case Study of Werewolves*
Joseph D. Reich — *Connecting the Dots to Shangrila*
Joseph D. Reich — *The Derivation of Cowboys and Indians*
Joseph D. Reich — *The Hole That Runs Through Utopia*
Joseph D. Reich — *The Housing Market*
Kenneth Rosen and Richard Wilson — *Gomorrah*
Fred Rosenblum — *Vietnumb*
David Schein — *My Murder and Other Local News*
Harold Schweizer — *Miriam's Book*
Scott T. Starbuck — *Carbonfish Blues*
Scott T. Starbuck — *Hawk on Wire*
Scott T. Starbuck — *Industrial Oz*
Seth Steinzor — *Among the Lost*
Seth Steinzor — *To Join the Lost*
Susan Thomas — *In the Sadness Museum*
Susan Thomas — *The Empty Notebook Interrogates Itself*
Paolo Valesio/Todd Portnowitz — *La Mezzanotte di Spoleto/Midnight in Spoleto*
Sharon Webster — *Everyone Lives Here*
Tony Whedon — *The Tres Riches Heures*
Tony Whedon — *The Falkland Quartet*
Claire Zoghb — *Dispatches from Everest*

Stories
Jay Boyer — *Flight*
L. M Brown — *Treading the Uneven Road*
Michael Cocchiarale — *Here Is Ware*
Michael Cocchiarale — *Still Time*
Neil Connelly — *In the Wake of Our Vows*
Catherine Zobal Dent — *Unfinished Stories of Girls*
Zdravka Evtimova — *Carts and Other Stories*
John Michael Flynn — *Off to the Next Wherever*
Derek Furr — *Semitones*
Derek Furr — *Suite for Three Voices*
Elizabeth Genovise — *Where There Are Two or More*
Andrei Guriuanu — *Body of Work*
Zeke Jarvis — *In A Family Way*

Fomite

Arya Jenkins — *Blue Songs in an Open Key*
Jan English Leary — *Skating on the Vertical*
Larry Lefkowitz — *Enigmatic Tales*
Marjorie Maddox — *What She Was Saying*
William Marquess — *Boom-shacka-lacka*
Gary Miller — *Museum of the Americas*
Jennifer Anne Moses — *Visiting Hours*
Martin Ott — *Interrogations*
Christopher Peterson — *Amoebic Simulacra*
Jack Pulaski — *Love's Labours*
Charles Rafferty — *Saturday Night at Magellan's*
Ron Savage — *What We Do For Love*
Fred Skolnik — *Americans and Other Stories*
Lynn Sloan — *This Far Is Not Far Enough*
L.E. Smith — *Views Cost Extra*
Caitlin Hamilton Summie — *To Lay To Rest Our Ghosts*
Susan Thomas — *Among Angelic Orders*
Tom Walker — *Signed Confessions*
Silas Dent Zobal — *The Inconvenience of the Wings*

Odd Birds
William Benton — *Eye Contact: Writing on Art*
Micheal Breiner — *the way none of this happened*
J. C. Ellefson — *Under the Influence: Shouting Out to Walt*
David Ross Gunn — *Cautionary Chronicles*
Andrei Guriuanu and Teknari — *The Darkest City*
Gail Holst-Warhaft — *The Fall of Athens*
Roger Lebovitz — *A Guide to the Western Slopes and the Outlying Area*
Roger Lebovitz — *Twenty-two Instructions for Near Survival*
dug Nap— *Artsy Fartsy*
Delia Bell Robinson — *A Shirtwaist Story*
Peter Schumann — *Belligerent & Not So Belligerent Slogans from the Possibilitarian Arsenal*
Peter Schumann — *Bread & Sentences*
Peter Schumann — *Charlotte Salomon*
Peter Schumann — *Diagonal Man, Volumes One and Two*
Peter Schumann — *Faust 3*
Peter Schumann — *Planet Kasper, Volumes One and Two*
Peter Schumann — *We*

Plays
Stephen Goldberg — *Screwed and Other Plays*
Michele Markarian — *Unborn Children of America*

Essays
Robert Sommer — *Losing Francis: Essays on the Wars at Home*
Robert Sommer — *Losing Francis: Essays on the Wars at Home*

www.ingramcontent.com/pod-product-compliance
Lightning Source LLC
Chambersburg PA
CBHW030158100526
44592CB00009B/344